My Fishing

Adventures

This Book Belongs To

_____

Catch of the Day

Date:	Location:
Bait/Lures:	
Fishing Buddies:	

Notes:

_____

_____

_____

_____

_____

Catch of the Day

Date:	Location:

Bait/Lures:

Fishing Buddies:

Notes:
_____
_____
_____
_____
_____

Catch of the Day

Date:	Location:

Bait/Lures:

Fishing Buddies:

Notes: _____

_____

_____

_____

_____

_____

Catch of the Day

Date:	Location:
Bait/Lures:	
Fishing Buddies:	

Notes:

_____

_____

_____

_____

_____

_____

Catch of the Day

Date:	Location:
Bait/Lures:	
Fishing Buddies:	

Notes:

_____

_____

_____

_____

_____

_____

Catch of the Day

Date:	Location:
Bait/Lures:	
Fishing Buddies:	

Notes:

_____

_____

_____

_____

_____

_____

Catch of the Day

Date:	Location:
Bait/Lures:	
Fishing Buddies:	

Notes: _____

_____

_____

_____

_____

_____

Catch of the Day

Date:	Location:
Bait/Lures:	
Fishing Buddies:	

Notes:

_____

_____

_____

_____

_____

Catch of the Day

Date:	Location:

Bait/Lures:

Fishing Buddies:

Notes:

Catch of the Day

Date:	Location:

Bait/Lures:

Fishing Buddies:

Notes:
_____

_____

_____

_____

_____

Catch of the Day

Date:	Location:

Bait/Lures:

Fishing Buddies:

Notes:

_____

_____

_____

_____

_____

Catch of the Day

Date:	Location:

Bait/Lures:

Fishing Buddies:

Notes:

_____

_____

_____

_____

_____

Catch of the Day

Date:	Location:

Bait/Lures:

Fishing Buddies:

Notes:

_____

_____

_____

_____

_____

_____

Catch of the Day

Date:	Location:

Bait/Lures:

Fishing Buddies:

Notes:

_____

_____

_____

_____

_____

Catch of the Day

Date:	Location:

Bait/Lures:

Fishing Buddies:

Notes:
_____
_____
_____
_____
_____

Catch of the Day

Date:	Location:
Bait/Lures:	
Fishing Buddies:	

Notes:

_____

_____

_____

_____

_____

_____

Catch of the Day

Date:	Location:

Bait/Lures:

Fishing Buddies:

Notes:

_____

_____

_____

_____

_____

Catch of the Day

Date:	Location:

Bait/Lures:

Fishing Buddies:

Notes:
_____

_____

_____

_____

_____

_____

Catch of the Day

Date:	Location:
Bait/Lures:	
Fishing Buddies:	

Notes:

_____

_____

_____

_____

_____

Catch of the Day

Date:	Location:

Bait/Lures:

Fishing Buddies:

Notes:

Catch of the Day

Date:	Location:

Bait/Lures:

Fishing Buddies:

Notes:

Catch of the Day

Date:	Location:
Bait/Lures:	
Fishing Buddies:	

Notes:
_____

_____

_____

_____

_____

Catch of the Day

Date:	Location:
Bait/Lures:	
Fishing Buddies:	

Notes:

_____

_____

_____

_____

_____

Catch of the Day

Date:	Location:

Bait/Lures:

Fishing Buddies:

Notes:

_____

_____

_____

_____

_____

Catch of the Day

Date:	Location:

Bait/Lures:

Fishing Buddies:

Notes:

_____

_____

_____

_____

_____

Catch of the Day

Date:	Location:

Bait/Lures:

Fishing Buddies:

Notes:

Catch of the Day

Date:	Location:

Bait/Lures:

Fishing Buddies:

Notes:

Catch of the Day

Date:	Location:

Bait/Lures:

Fishing Buddies:

Notes: _____

_____

_____

_____

_____

_____

Catch of the Day

Date:	Location:
Bait/Lures:	
Fishing Buddies:	

Notes:

_____

_____

_____

_____

_____

_____

Catch of the Day

Date:	Location:
Bait/Lures:	
Fishing Buddies:	

Notes:

_____

_____

_____

_____

_____

_____

Catch of the Day

Date:	Location:

Bait/Lures:

Fishing Buddies:

Notes:

Catch of the Day

Date:	Location:

Bait/Lures:

Fishing Buddies:

Notes:

Catch of the Day

Date:	Location:
Bait/Lures:	
Fishing Buddies:	

Notes:

Catch of the Day

Date:	Location:
Bait/Lures:	
Fishing Buddies:	

Notes:

_____

_____

_____

_____

_____

_____

Catch of the Day

Date:	Location:

Bait/Lures:

Fishing Buddies:

Notes:

Catch of the Day

Date:	Location:

Bait/Lures:

Fishing Buddies:

Notes:

Catch of the Day

Date:	Location:
Bait/Lures:	
Fishing Buddies:	

Notes:

_____

_____

_____

_____

_____

_____

Catch of the Day

Date:	Location:
Bait/Lures:	
Fishing Buddies:	

Notes:

_____

_____

_____

_____

_____

_____

Catch of the Day

Date:	Location:
Bait/Lures:	
Fishing Buddies:	

Notes:

_____

_____

_____

_____

_____

Catch of the Day

Date:	Location:

Bait/Lures:

Fishing Buddies:

Notes:

Catch of the Day

Date:	Location:

Bait/Lures:

Fishing Buddies:

Notes:

Catch of the Day

Date:	Location:
Bait/Lures:	
Fishing Buddies:	

Notes:

_____

_____

_____

_____

_____

_____

Catch of the Day

Date:	Location:

Bait/Lures:

Fishing Buddies:

Notes:
_____

_____

_____

_____

_____

_____

Catch of the Day

Date:	Location:
Bait/Lures:	
Fishing Buddies:	

Notes:

_____

_____

_____

_____

_____

Catch of the Day

Date:	Location:

Bait/Lures:

Fishing Buddies:

Notes:

Catch of the Day

Date:	Location:

Bait/Lures:

Fishing Buddies:

Notes:

_____

_____

_____

_____

_____

_____

Catch of the Day

Date:	Location:
Bait/Lures:	
Fishing Buddies:	

Notes:

_____

_____

_____

_____

_____

_____

Catch of the Day

Date:	Location:
Bait/Lures:	
Fishing Buddies:	

Notes:

_____

_____

_____

_____

_____

_____

Made in the USA
Columbia, SC
25 October 2018